Divinely Inspired Messages from the Heart

"Just stay in God's Word and study da 'Good Book'!"

—Jan D. Johnson

Divinely Inspired Messages from the Heart

Dr. Jan Darice Johnson

Copyright

Copyright © 2016 by Dr. Jan Darice Johnson. All rights reserved. This book or any portion thereof may not be reproduced or used in any manner whatsoever without the express written permission of The Butterfly Typeface Publishing House Co. except for the use of brief quotations in a book review.

Scripture quotations taken from the 21st Century King James Version @, copyright 1994. Used by permission of Deuel Enterprises, Inc., Gary, SD 57237. All rights reserved.

Printed in the United States of America

First Printing, 2016

ISBN-13: 978-1-942022-38-1

Illustrations by Ashley Renee / Abstract Designz

The Butterfly Typeface Publishing
PO BOX 56193
Little Rock, Arkansas 72215

Dedication

It is with honor that I dedicate *Divinely Inspired Messages from the Heart* to my parents, Darius and Janie Johnson, who are now deceased. You taught me so many lessons in life, and for that, I will be eternally grateful! Your love for God was reflected in all that you did.

You always inspired me to strive to do my best! You supported my creativity and encouraged me to "reach for the stars!" Although you are not physically here today, I know that you are with me in spirit and that you will continue to be my "cheerleaders from Heaven!"

Momma and Daddy, I will always love you, and I will never forget you!

I also dedicate this book to my future grandchildren, my great grandchildren, and my great, great grandchildren. It is my prayer that they will come to know God personally and that they will trust Him to guide them always.

"Giving praise, glory, and honor to God is significant when one can witness God's awesomeness through the 'gifts' and 'talents' in which He has blessed us."

- Dr. Jan D Johnson

Table of Contents

Intimacies

My Husband 24

My Children 27

My Family 30

Welcome Little Son! 32

Beautiful Daughter! 33

Gratitude

Do You Remember? 38

God Is… 39

Isn't It Amazing? 42

Lord, You Know… 43

Gratitude 44

Blessings

Sunshine 46

Rain 47

Beautiful Flowers 49

Summer Is Fun... 51

It's Christmas... 53

Legacies

Sisters.. 58

My Sorors Of UKO 61

DOTK 62

True Friends... 64

Some People 65

Inspiration

Don't Forget... 69

God Is There! 70

Missing You! 71

Challenges Of Life 73

Prayer 74

Love

Forgiveness 76

God's Love 77

Jesus, I Love You! 78

Dearly Beloved 81

Accolades

Climbin' Da Mountain 85

Teachers 90

Firefighters 93

Military Tribute 97

Me, The Poet	100
My Custom Symbol	101
About The Author	105
Scripture Reference	107

Foreword

During my high school days, I was blessed to have the same science teacher three of the four years. He encouraged his students each day to do their best. He was methodical and systematic in his instructions.

The teacher that I am referring to is Mr. Darius Johnson, the father of the author, Dr. Jan Johnson. During the time in which I did not have classes under him, I made it my duty to visit his classroom in our spare time for leadership and inspiration. When I attended undergraduate school, my relationship with Mr. Johnson continued.

My first step to honor his influence was to enroll in college as a chemistry major. The Johnson family lived within walking distance from the university, and we spent many evenings fellowshipping. Years later, I became pastor of the church in which the Johnson family was in membership, and Mr. Johnson was one of the leaders.

Presently, six of our high school classmates sponsor a Bible conference. Many of the topics discussed are family relationship values that Mr. Darius Johnson taught and practiced.

The works of Dr. Jan Johnson on family relationships are a welcomed resource to attitudes and inspiration, as well as our immediate family. I find that these readings are reflections of the family values she has experienced and are a welcomed guide to family relationships. I find ample cause to commend this fine work to every believer.

Rev. Dr. Ivory E. Swann, Pastor
Second Missionary Baptist Church

Foreword

In our hectic, fast-paced world, seldom do we take time to reflect on what is most important in our lives. We hurry through our morning routines, shove the kids off to school, gulp down a cup of caffeine, and dive right into bumper-to-bumper traffic, rushing off to give our very best to a job or career that often leaves us feeling empty.

There is no time for a kind word to encourage our loved ones in their day. We have no time for a tender parting moment with our mate.

We rush through precious moments and valuable life experiences, taking for granted that our loved ones know how we feel about them, taking for granted that they will be there when we return home, and taking for granted that the next day, or even the next moment, is promised to us.

This book is not that way. In *Divinely Inspired Messages from the Heart*, Dr. Jan Johnson shares her heartfelt love and appreciation for what's most important in her life—her love for God, her love for family and friends, and her appreciation for the things in life that we often take for granted.

As a dedicated wife, mother, daughter, sister, career woman, and friend, Jan has experienced just enough joy and pain in her life to mold her heart into a vessel that God can use. Through simple words and abundant faith, she has placed her gift of words into the hands of God.

May this gift be a blessing to your life, your marriage, and your family. We pray that Dr. Johnson's gift of poetry is a reminder of what is truly important in your life.

Reverends Sammy & Sonya Shropshire
Marriage Ministers
Wood Memorial Chapel Gospel Congregation
Fort Bragg, North Carolina

Acknowledgement

I would like to acknowledge my family who has supported me throughout this book writing endeavor. My husband, Robert Johnson, encouraged and supported my poetry writing. He was brutally honest with his critiques, because he only wanted me to produce my best writing. "Robert, thank you for believing in me and for encouraging my worth."

To my children, Robert II and Robyn, "You were always there as gentle encouragers, and you always told me how proud you were of me for moving forward with my poetry writing efforts. Your support inspired me to keep going so that I could reach this goal."

"Thank you, Mom and Dad, for planting the seed! Thank you, Robert, Robyn, and Robert II for sharing in the watering process as you assisted me to blossom to my fullest potential as a writer. I love and appreciate you all very much!"

"Thank you to my Pastor, Rev. Dr. Ivory Swann, for your Biblical teachings and for your support of my book through your foreword message."

Reverends Sammy and Sonya Shropshire, "Thank you for your encouragement and loving support when I needed it most. I will never forget you."

Introduction

All of these poems are original and were divinely inspired, thus the title, *Divinely Inspired Messages from the Heart.*

God is truly the source of my inspiration and creativity; without Him, there would be no poetry at all. Each poem reflects my love and adoration for Him and has a special message for the readers.

My husband, children, and family were also sources of inspiration for these poems.

My husband has personally witnessed the power of prayer. He knows that there is nothing that God cannot do! My husband is my helpmate and my best friend. I thank God for him every day!

My children are true blessings from God. They are mighty in God, and they believe in the power of prayer. They are supportive of each other and their parents too! They love each other unconditionally, and we love them unconditionally as well.

Our family is not very large, but we are very blessed to have each other. We know God and the miracles that we have witnessed. Some of us are prayer warriors, which helps to keep our family together. We enjoy family gatherings, the fellowship, food, and fun.

Even with our differences, we are all God's children!

Intimacies

*The poem, My Husband,
is dedicated to my husband, Robert!
"Thank you for 34 wonderful years!"*

My Husband

My husband is a wonderful man.

He provides for our family

and tries to help others the best that he can.

No matter what the task, he works extremely hard.

His favorite place to be is working outside in the yard.

But don't you dare think

that he ignores the dirty dishes in the sink.

He definitely knows his way around the kitchen.

There are many dishes that he prepares which range from

vegetables, steak, pastries, and chicken.

Life for us hasn't always been grand.

Yet through all of our tests and trials, my best friend and I,

together we stand.

I love my husband, I surely do.

The love we share is genuine and true!

There is no other man on this earth,

who supports me and always encourages my worth.

My husband is always there!

The love we have for each other,

we will forever share.

*The poem, My Children,
is dedicated to my children,
Robert II and Robyn,
whom I will always love!*

My Children

My daughter and my son are very special to me!

I remember when they were very young,

no danger could they see.

They climbed on just about everything

without even a flinch.

But they always looked to dad and mom

to get them out of a pinch.

They ran around throughout the house,

and rarely were they as quiet as a mouse.

Being quiet all the time was not their way,

and they always enjoyed going outside to play.

In school, they always tried their best,

and when it came to friendships, they passed the test.

Even now as adults, their friends will come through,

and they always reminisce about the days of their youth.

They often talk of the "good old days,"

as life took them through a magical maze.

I love my children, yes I do!

My love for them will always be true!

My Family

Do you know how special my family is to me?

Well, keep reading and the answer you will soon receive...

F-Faithfully standing by my side.

A-Always willing to lend a helping hand.

M-Mirroring God's love in all that they do.

I-Including prayer in their daily lives too.

L-Loyally and lovingly supporting each other every step of the way.

Y-Yearning for none to perish, wanting us all to be saved!

There is no greater gift than the gift of FAMILY.

This is why my family is so special to me!

Both poems *Welcome Little Son* and *Beautiful Daughter* were inspired by the births of our own children, Robyn and Robert II.

God blessed Robert and me with our beautiful, loving, and Godly children, and we cherish our precious gifts from God. God blessed them to be healthy and "normal."

They are blessed to have the activity of their limbs, five fingers, and five toes. They are enclosed in their right minds, and they have the blessings of God's favor on their lives. He has entrusted our children's lives to us, and we are charged to raise them in the admonition of the Lord.

The Lord said in **Proverbs 22:6 (NKJV)** that we should "Train up a child in the way he should go, and when he is old he will not depart from it."

"God, please know that we have done our best to raise our children Your way and with Your guidance!"

Welcome Little Son!

Congratulations on the birth of your precious infant son.

I am sure you are thankful to God for your healthy,

little one.

For only God knows the path he will take.

You, as his parents will help guide the decisions

that he will make.

Love him and train him in the way that he should go.

I know his Heavenly Father, you will teach him to know.

Share God's goodness, love, and His Word,

with your son each and every day.

If you're faithful in doing this, your son will grow up

to love God, and His Word, he will obey.

Beautiful Daughter!

Hello little daughter! I am glad that you are finally here.
Carrying you was only 9 months,
but at times, it seemed like a whole year.
I finally get to hold you in my arms.
Not only am I admiring your beauty, but I am mesmerized by
your God-given charm.
I am grateful to God
that you are as perfect as can be.
You have two eyes, two ears, two legs, two feet, five toes,
a cute little nose and much more;
so I am happy.
I continually thank God
for your perfect little body!
Lord, help me as I raise her,
to be what You would have her to be.
I will be forever grateful for this beautiful "gift" of which You
have blessed me.
My desire is for her to love and to cherish You, God,
as much as I do.
I want her to love You forever, and to You be eternally true!

Gratitude

The poems, *Do You Remember?*, *God Is …*, *Isn't it Amazing?*, *Lord You Know*, and *Dearly Beloved* were inspired by the fact that God sent His only Son, Jesus, to die on the cross at Calvary to save us from sin. His purpose was so that you and I might have an opportunity to live eternally with Christ.

Jesus knew us, but His Father knew us well! God loved us so much that He was willing to sacrifice the life of His only Son so that we might be free. Were we really a friend to Jesus when He was destined to die on the cross? Jesus suffered ridicule from the crowds and faced hostile name calling. People spat on him. He endured brutal beatings and yet, Jesus bravely followed through with His plight by dying on the cross.

John 15:13 (KJV) Greater love hath no man than this, that a man lay down his life for his friends.

Today, are we staying in God's Word, following His commands, treating our fellowman with love? No, there is no greater love! "Thank you, God, for Your Son, The Sacrificial Lamb!" "Thank you, Jesus, for making the ultimate sacrifice!"

Although we can never repay Him for the sacrifice He made on Calvary or for His unconditional love and devotion to us, there are a few things that we can do.

(1.) Diligently seek Him.

(2.) Live a life that represents Christ.

(3.) Obey God's Word.

(4.) Love one another as God has loved us.

(5.) Know and believe in your heart that God loves you and know that He always keeps His Word.

(6.) Engage in fervent prayer.

Thank you!

        Thank you!

                Thank you!

Do You Remember?

Lord, how can I forget all the things

You've done in my life?

You healed me, when I never thought I would be.

You answered my prayers,

and the answers came right on time.

You saved me when I was lost in sin.

Right on time, You stepped in.

You guide my life each and every day...

because without You, there is no other way.

If it wasn't for Your grace, mercy,

and Your loving kindness,

I don't know where I would be!

Do I remember? Yes, I do!

God Is...

God is Alpha and Omega ...

The Beginning and The End.

God is my Strength when...

I have exhausted all of mine.

God is my Friend...

When all others forsake me.

God is my Father and Mother...

Now that my earthly parents are no longer with me.

God is my Joy...

That no one can take away.

God is my Stability...

In a world full of turmoil.

God is my Peace...

In the midst of a treacherous storm.

God is my Guiding Light...

When all around me, darkness I see.

God is my Hope...

When there seems to be none at all.

God is my Comforter....

Just when I need Him most.

God is my All and All....

Above Him there is no other!

My God Is Awesome!

Isn't It Amazing?

Isn't it amazing how the seasons change.
or how quickly the weather goes from sunshine to rain?

Isn't it amazing how quickly children grow,
from little infants drinking milk to adults who can eat it all, you know!

Isn't it amazing how flowers grow,
from little seeds planted in the ground buried under the snow.

Isn't it amazing how God's only son died way back on Calvary?
Yes, Jesus gave His life, so that you and I could be free.

Isn't it amazing how Jesus shed His blood for lowly you and me?
If He had not done this, I would hate to think where we would be.

Isn't It Amazing?

Isn't it amazing how the seasons change,

or how quickly the weather goes from sunshine to rain?

Isn't it amazing how quickly children grow,

from little infants drinking milk to adults who can eat it all,

you know!

Isn't it amazing how flowers grow,

from little seeds planted in the ground

buried under the snow?

Isn't it amazing how God's only Son died,

way back on Calvary?

Yes, Jesus gave His life, so that you and I could be free.

Isn't it amazing how Jesus shed His blood

for lowly you and me?

If He had not done this,

I would hate to think where we would be.

Lord, You Know...

Lord, You know my thoughts

and whether or not they are clean.

Help me Father, in my actions, not to be mean.

Lord, You know my mind

of which all of my actions are inclined.

Help me to strive to be to others always kind.

Lord, You know me, and You did before I knew myself.

So whatever I do, let it be pleasing to You.

Whatever I say, Dear God, guide my words, so I say them,

the right way.

Lord, You know that I am Your child, and I will always be,

because my ultimate goal after death is to live with You

in Heaven eternally.

Gratitude

Heavenly Father, I cannot express my gratitude enough

for all You've done for me.

You're my Life, my Strength and my Hope for all eternally.

You know my past, my present, my future, and

my destiny You can see.

In You, I will always trust.

Lord, You so unselfishly gave

Your Son's life for us.

Jesus willingly sacrificed His life for you and me,

by dying on Calvary's tree.

What greater joy! Grateful to Him, I will always be.

My love for You and my gratitude will last for all eternity.

Blessings

Sunshine

The sun is shining brightly today.

I have joy in my heart,

no matter whatever may come my way!

The flowers dance in the sun's beautiful rays.

The people rejoice, "It's a beautiful, sunny day!"

The children can finally play outside!

They are running, jumping, and turning

with their arms open wide.

What fun they are having, as they shout with glee….

"What a beautiful, sunny day! Isn't it heavenly?"

Rain

Rain is just God's way to refresh the air.
It will get rid of impurities that dwell there.
Rain is God's way of making things grow,
The flowers, grass and trees...people too, you know.

Rain is a part of the water cycle that goes around.
First, rain evaporates from a source, next it condenses,
and finally, it falls from the sky to the ground.

Rain, at times, comes in the forms of snow or ice.
Contrary to popular belief, it can often fall where you live
more than twice.

Rain can cause problems when it comes too much.
It can cause flooding, erosion, street closings, and such!

It's a blessing when it rains after a long drought!
The rain comes right on time,
to help the inhabitants of the earth out!

Thank God for the rain!

Beautiful Flowers

Beautiful flowers are blooming everywhere.
The sweet fragrance of the blossoms completely permeates the air.

Spring is a welcomed season each year.
Nature's new life begins and that's a sure sign that summer is very near.

Dogwood trees bloom and the lily comes,
More and more roses appear and so do the mums.

Look at the splendor of God's mighty work!
Even in the cracks and crevices, the ivy will lurk.
Beautiful flowers, each with an awesome smell.
Which ones to pick from the garden?
The decision is difficult because I love them all so well.

The stained glass vase on my dining room table looks so amazing there.
I sit and gaze at the beauty from my dining room chair.

Each flower has been touched by God's Holy hand.
Tiny hummingbirds fluttering by and the bumblebees buzzing as on each flower they land.
Each of these helps the flower grow and each is a part of God's plan.

There is so much that we don't know
About what makes each seed into a flower grow.

The beautiful flowers that we see,
Come from God and Him only!!!

Divinely Inspired Messages from The Heart

Beautiful Flowers

Beautiful flowers are blooming everywhere.

The sweet fragrance of the blossoms completely

permeates the air.

Spring is a welcomed season each year.

Nature's new life begins, and that's a sure sign

that summer is very near.

Dogwood trees bloom, and the lily comes,

more and more roses appear, and so do the mums.

Look at the splendor of God's mighty work!

Even in the cracks and crevices, the ivy will lurk.

Beautiful flowers, each with an awesome smell.

Which ones to pick from the garden?

The decision is difficult, because I love them so well.

The stained-glass vase on my dining room table

looks so amazing there.

I sit and gaze at the beauty from my dining room chair.

Each flower has been touched by God's holy hand.

Tiny hummingbirds fluttering by, and the bumblebees

buzzing as on each flower they land.

Each of these helps the flower grow,

and each is a part of God's plan.

There is so much that we don't know

about what makes each seed into a flower grow.

The beautiful flowers that we see,

come from God and Him only!

Summer Is Fun

S-Summer is Fun!

U-Umbrellas are open, and grills are everywhere.

M-Mothers at the park with their children, as they play and swing through the air.

M-Meadows filled with daffodils swaying in the breeze.

E-Everything seems alive, all of God's creation: the flowers, grass, birds, the people, and even the trees.

R- Racers are on their bikes vying to win the races.

F- Fathers in the backyard, gently tossing balls and protecting their children from getting accidently hit in their faces

U-Uber drivers are all over the place, vowing to keep their passengers safe.

N-No one is sad! Happiness everywhere!

Summer is Fun!

Divinely Inspired Messages from The Heart

The poem, *It's Christmas*, reflects upon one of my favorite times of the year. The hustle and bustle of the season is magical! People are shopping, and there is laughter in the air. Families are planning gatherings with lots of food and fun! Loved ones are coming from near and far to spend time together. Merriment is all around! Trees are being decorated, and lights are strung all around the house! Oh, how pretty everything looks, and the many festive fragrances permeate the air.

One thing that we can't forget in all of the excitement is the reason for the season! Jesus was born to Mary and Joseph in a manger in Bethlehem. He was and continues to be the "Savior of the world!" I can only imagine the stressfulness that surrounded His birth. His mother and father were searching for lodging so that Mary could rest and deliver her infant son. There was nowhere for them to go but to a lowly stable, where the animals lived. A feeding trough was his bassinet!

Unfortunately, the world didn't know that this little baby was a King! He was deserving of the best, and yet, He received the least. Too bad they didn't know that He would grow up to win wayward souls for His Father, God's kingdom! Wow...they didn't realize that Jesus's birth was significant and that His death would be even more so!

Have you ever thought, "What if Jesus had not been born? Who would go to Calvary to stand in our stead? Who would save us and set us free?"

Thank God for Jesus!

It's Christmas

It's Christmas time!

The family gathers around the beautifully decorated tree,

singing lots of carols, drinking hot chocolate, and awaiting

Santa's arrival very patiently.

But what about baby Jesus and the wonder of His birth?

Don't they know that His birth was the most

miraculous on earth?

He was born in a lowly manger,

but Mary and Joseph protected Him from danger.

The Three Wise Men came to see,

the special, little baby.

They brought many gifts, spices, and much more,

for the little baby the world would one day adore.

When we celebrate Christmas, we must not forget

that the reason we celebrate is the best one yet.

Jesus, the Son of God, was born in a manger far away.

That's why we celebrate Christmas Day.

But His purpose in life was to set us all free,

so that with Him one day we can live eternally.

Legacies

The poem, *Sisters*, is dedicated to my birth sister, Berta! Berta and I were born to my now deceased parents, Darius and Janie Johnson. We were born 15 months apart.

Our parents gave us a wonderful life that others could only dream of having. I realized then and know now that our parents were true blessings from God. They sacrificed so much, so that my sister and I would have a good life. I am grateful for the example of God's love that my parents showed us each day.

Now that Berta and I are left to carry on the legacy of love that our parents left to us, we must realize how special our sisterly relationship is and how we too must love each other as God loves us! We should appreciate each other and show that appreciation as often as we can.

We both have children now, and the example of love that was shown by our loving parents must now be passed on to our children.

"I love you my dear sister!"

Sisters

Sisters are as special as they can be.

They are a vital part of the family.

When you need a friend to lean on, they are there for you,

and always wondering in their minds

what else can they do.

They offer their love and advice

whether you ask for it or not.

Everything they do for you

always comes from the heart.

What would we do without our sisters,

for their love is really true.

Without a sister's love,

can you imagine what you would do?

The poem *My Sorors of UKO* is written about a group of women who are truly bonded together through our "sisterhood!" We have in the past and continue to work together for "service to all mankind!" The love we have for each other is very special, and we truly care about the welfare of each soror.

I also have a family of sisters who have "informally adopted" me as their sister. We do a lot of things together, and they love me as if I was really their sister. We have established a bond; love is the foundation of our relationship. We cry together, laugh together, and wish only the best for each other. Although we are not really sisters, we are indeed "sisters in Christ"! "Thank you, my sisters, for your love!"

"I love you all!"

John 13:34-35 - A new commandment I give unto you, That ye love one another; as I have loved you, that ye also love one another.

Proverbs 3:17 (KJV) - Her ways are ways of pleasantness, and all her paths are peace.

Matthew 12:50 (KJV) - For whosoever shall do the will of my Father which is in heaven, the same is my brother, and sister, and mother.

My Sorors of UKO

My UKO Sorors are special to me.
They care about my well being with sincerity.

During Community Service Projects they always give their all.
They are willing and available for the service call.

My UKO Sorors are the best!
Of all the other sororities, we certainly outshine the rest.

Our sisterhood is a special one,
Because above ours, there is none.

From "Shopping with the Sheriff" to the Bicycle Man Giveways",
We have a lot of projects to fill our days.

No matter what issues my come our way,
Through our prayers and trust in God, we can face them, come what may!

I am telling you this simply because it is so,
There are no others like my Sorors of UKO!

Soror Jan D. Johnson

My Sorors of UKO

My UKO Sorors are special to me.
They care about my well-being with sincerity.
During Community Service Projects,
they always give their all.
They are willing and available for the service call.
My UKO Sorors are the best!
Of all the other sororities, we certainly outshine the rest.
Our sisterhood is a special one,
because above ours, there is none.
From "Shopping with the Sheriff"
to the "Bicycle Man Giveaways",
we have a lot of projects to fill our days.
No matter what issues come our way,
through our prayers and trust in God,
we can face them, come, what may!
I am telling you this simply because it is so,
there are no others like my Sorors of UKO!

DOTK

"Daughters of the King"

DOTK, we are sisters through our relationship with God,
for on holy ground we carefully trod.

We're not saying that He belongs exclusively to us,
but in God, we faithfully place all of our trust!

When we need a few kind words, a smile,
a big hug, or a prayer,
my sisters of DOTK are unselfishly there.
They are always showing how much they care.

Through our many talents and gifts
of which we are blessed,
we praise and thank God, as we give Him our best.

We realize that without God, we are hopelessly lost.
We are eternally grateful that Jesus died for us,
and paid the ultimate cost.

We are so happy that Jesus has set us free!
We thank God daily for sending His only Son
to die for us on Calvary.

For through Jesus, God's Son, we have the opportunity
to live with God eternally.

DOTK, we will always be
giving God the highest praise
and our utmost glory!

Galatians 3:26 (KJV) "For ye are all the children of God by faith in Christ Jesus."

Revelation 19:6-7(KJV) 6. And I heard as it were the voice of a great multitude, and as the voice of many waters, and as the voice of mighty thunderings, saying, Hallelujah! For the Lord God Almighty reigns. 7. Let us rejoice and be glad and give him glory! For the wedding of the Lamb has come, and his bride has made herself ready.

True Friends

True friends are like rainbows.

They come in all beautiful colors, shapes, and sizes.

Their love for you shows, so now everyone knows.

True friends are there when you need them and even

when you don't.

They encourage you and support you

even when all others won't.

They are always ready to comfort you and

lend a listening ear...

And they will let you know when away from negativity you

should always steer.

There is always joy and laughter

when true friends are around,

so if everyone is laughing, there is no room for a frown.

True friends are special. They mean everything to me.

True friends are rarely found,

so that is why I cherish them, you see!

Some People

Some people are very nice and are always very happy.

Some people are really grumpy and never wear a smile.

Some people dress very well,

and love to shop…. you can tell.

Some people really don't care

about the clothes they decide to wear.

Some people know about Jesus,

The One who died for you and me.

Jesus, who gave His life on Calvary,

so that we all could be free.

Some people don't care to know,

just how much Jesus loves us so.

Some people have accepted God's call,

for a new life with Him through salvation,

it's simple … that's all.

Some people choose not to change;

their lives they don't wish to rearrange.

Some people know the way to go,

because there is no doubt Jesus loves them so.

Some people will share this news with others….

their friends, uncles, aunts, mothers, dads,

sisters, and brothers.

Some people wish for all to be free,

so they can live together with Jesus eternally.

Inspiration

The Poems *Don't Forget, God Is There* and *I'm Missing You* are poems of faith, trust, hope, comfort, and encouragement. Adversities will come into our lives, but we don't have to succumb to them. **Deuteronomy 31:6 (KJV)** Be strong and of a good courage, fear not, nor be afraid of them: for the LORD thy God, he *it is* that doth go with thee; he will not fail thee, nor forsake thee.

Loneliness is an emotion that we may feel sometimes, but don't forget that we are not alone. God is always with us and never leaves our sides. **Deuteronomy 31:8 (KJV)** And the LORD, he *it i*s that doth go before thee; he will be with thee, he will not fail thee, neither forsake thee: fear not, neither be dismayed.

When we are heartbroken or sad, turn that sadness or broken heartedness into happiness because Christ has set us free. He gave His life so that we could have life and have it bountifully. God is with us as a comforter, and He is only a prayer away. When we feel that we cannot go on and there is absolutely no way out, trust that God sees and He knows all things. **John 10:10 (KJV)** [1] The thief cometh not, but for to steal, and to kill, and to destroy: I am come that they might have life, and that they might have it more abundantly. He can make a way out of what seems to be a hopeless situation. God can turn things around in your life to work in your favor, but we must trust Him.

Don't Forget

Have you ever felt that there was absolutely no way out,

and your life seemed to be tossed about?

Don't forget God is always there;

seek Him diligently in fervent prayer.

When you try with all your might,

but it seems as if you are losing the fight,

forge ahead; be strong.

The coming of your breakthrough won't be long.

Stop, don't shed a tear.

Dry your eyes, have no fear...for your Heavenly Father

is always near!

When the weight of the world makes you feel like on your

face you will land,

don't forget... God has you

and He holds you in the palm of His hand.

God Is There!

When you are hurting deep inside

and all you seem to do is cry,

don't forget who has your back; no matter what,

God is there.

Don't you dare consider giving up,

because God really does care!

He sees all, He knows all, and He is everywhere!

It is true that He will hear you,

if you whisper a little prayer?

God is there for you, no matter the situation.

Aren't you happy that He never takes

an unexpected vacation?

So dry your eyes, cheer up, and happily go about your day!

You can rest assured that God is with you

every step of the way.

Missing You!

Honey, I find myself missing you.

I miss everything about you, from the look in your eyes

to the smile on your face.

Yes, it's true, I'm missing you.

You left one day and told me you were on your way

to another place, and there you would stay.

Now that you're gone, what do I do?

Although I try so desperately not to,

I find myself missing you!

The phone calls are few,

and the text messages go unanswered.

Without communication, what will I do?

Being alone is difficult, it's true.

This loneliness does not go away! Boy, I am missing you!

But I soon remember, that my God I must seek.

He is my Comforter when I feel lonely and weak.

As always, He will see me through.

Yes, I need God's comfort,

because I am truly missing you!

Challenges of Life

We all face challenges every day,
but how do we handle it, when our lives are in disarray?

Do we scream? Do we yell?
Do we tell those all around us to go to Hell?

Do we cry? Are we sad?
Do we say mean things to make others mad?

Are we quiet? Do we pray?
Do we trust God to handle whatever comes our way?

Challenges in our lives may seem huge
or maybe even small.
We must remember that there is someone greater than us
who can handle them all!

God is always there! If we seek Him, He may be found!
He's the Greatest Problem Solver around!

God will patiently lead and guide you through
your challenges of life.
He will do it ever so gently, and there will be no strife.

God is waiting to answer your call.
Give the challenges to Him...He wants them all!

He will help you with each challenge you will face.
You couldn't put them in a better place.

Rest assured your challenges will flee.
Then you can give God all the glory!

Prayer

Prayer is something that I do,

in an effort to communicate with You!

In the morning when I wake-up to a beautiful new day,

Throughout the day I ask for Your protection and guidance

as I go about my way.

At night before I go to bed, I thank You for your blessings

and request Your watchful eye as I rest my head and

close my eyes to sleep.

"Thank You, God, for answering prayers

and for all You do for me!"

Prayer really works,

just try it and you'll see

that this form of communication is the best of all...

I'm sure you will agree!

Love

Forgiveness

Forgiveness is not always easy,
but with God's help, it can be done.

Your heart has been broken. It's difficult to go on,
but your strength comes from our Heavenly Father.
He is the Only One!

Forgiveness!

You're lost in your own pity,
and you don't know what to do.
My God can help you.
He is always there waiting too.

Forgiveness!

Depressed and hopeless, feeling all alone,
this is not a problem for God's only Son.
Just trust Him, and rest assured,
that the battle is already won!

Forgiveness!

Heavenly Father,
please forgive us for forgetting to turn to You.
We know that during our times of weakness,
only You can see us through.

Forgiveness!

God's Love

I want to show God's love each day,

and positively touch someone's life along the way.

I'll lovingly lend a listening ear,

and reassure someone who is uncertain,

that God is always near.

God shows His love at all times.

He wakes us up to see a new day.

He gives us strength to go along the way.

He lovingly guides us so that in His path

we will always stay.

God's love is unconditional!

There are no limits or stipulations.

God's love never fails.

Jesus, I Love You!

I love you Jesus, yes I do!

From the very beginning, Your love has always been true!

As God's only Son,

Your purpose in life

was predestined on earth.

Your purpose was spreading Your Father's Word

to all and sharing

God's worth.

Your mother and father were specifically chosen for You.

Their task was not easy,

but they knew what they had to do.

Born of a virgin,

what a miraculous conception!

The place of Your birth was nowhere near perfection.

From humble beginnings,

You started Your life.

What You endured throughout were trials,

tribulations, hatred,

and strife.

I thank You more than You will ever know.

The lives You have touched, the love You have given,

in You I will grow!

You lived Your life as an example for others.

You gave your life for all of Your sisters and brothers.

Dearly Beloved

Dearly Beloved, Your love is forever true,

and I wouldn't exist without You.

Dearly Beloved, You have my heart in Your hands.

Guide my life, and for You, I will always stand!

Dearly Beloved, show me the way!

Keep me in Your path day by day!

Dearly Beloved, to You each day I pray...

for Your grace and mercy, family, and friends.

Lord keep us, and guide us every day.

Dearly Beloved, eternally grateful I will always be!

Thank You for shedding your blood for me out on Calvary!

Dearly Beloved, I want You to know,

that my love for You I will always show!

Accolades

I was inspired to write the poem *Climbin' Da Mountain* in remembrance of "Black History" and in remembrance of our ancestors who have gone before us. Remembering that many of our ancestors were illiterate, but their faith in God was strong. Remembering that life for our ancestors was not easy way back then, and yet, being a Christian is not easy today.

There will be adversities that we will encounter, obstacles that seem to block our way, and unwarranted hostility towards us. Nevertheless, the saving grace is trusting and knowing, without a doubt, that God is with us every step of the way.

In Matthew 28:20 (KJV) God said, "Teaching them to observe all things whatsoever I have commanded you; and, lo, I am with you always, even unto the end of the world. Amen."

If we pray and are steadfast in God's Word, have faith and earnestly trust Him, we will make it to Heaven, which is our ultimate reward!

Climbin' Da Mountain

Climbin' da mountain ain't easy,
but you must keep a'climbin'… don't stop!
There's a reward a'waitin' when you reach da top!

You ask, "What's da reward? My answer
…. it's eternal life with da Lord!
If you trust God and obey His Word,
He will lead you there with little strife,
so you can have a joy filled life!

Although you know da paths are many to get there,
don't miss out
'cause all of your actions you will be aware.

Be careful of da path you take,
for only you can control da decisions you make.

Your choices are few….
God or da world.
Believe it or not da choice is up to you.

Just stay in God's Word and study da "Good Book"!
When you finally get to Heaven, you'll be happy
about your decisions and da path you took!

Climbin' da mountain ain't easy, but a great
reward awaits!

Teachers

Fire Fighters

Military

Teachers and Firefighters are the most needed, and yet in many cities, they are the lowest paid professionals. When I think about these two professions, I often wonder why their salaries are not commensurate with their many required duties...

Teachers' duties are extensive, and their performance expectations are often overwhelming. They prepare children and adults for life in the future.

All who are educated were taught by a teacher and have them to thank for preparing them for their professions whether as a lawyer, full or part-time student, teacher, preacher, doctor, dentist, astronaut, computer technologist, telecommunications specialist, firefighter, or whatever the profession.

There was a teacher who prepared you for life ahead. Teachers were there when you couldn't read a single word or could only write one letter. They were there when you had no understanding at all, and they consistently worked with you and supported you to ensure that you finally understood.

When you had a problem and couldn't solve it on your own, your teacher was the one who you turned to, and he/she helped you to work through your problems, whether they were academic, social or personal issues. "Stay in school and learn all that you can. One day your knowledge and expertise will be in great demand!"

Teachers

Teachers are very special people.
They are always there encouraging and supporting you.

Teachers come in all shapes, colors, and sizes.
They are full of love and share lots of surprises.

Learning for some does not come with ease,
but with the right teacher, learning is a breeze!

A willing spirit is all that teachers need,
and with God's help, they are bound to succeed.

I am a teacher, so I am telling you what I know.
Knowledge is power.
The more you know, the higher you will go.

Stay in school and learn all that you can.
One day your knowledge and expertise
will be in great demand.

Thank a teacher when the reading of this poem is done; you couldn't have done it without them….
TEACHERS, there are no others like them under the sun!

Firefighters

Fires can be fierce and they have such a treacherous, yet colorful glow...

which makes the job of a firefighter very challenging you know.

Firefighters battle fires on land and in the air, for flying high would give me such a

horrible scare. They seem to fight fires with such expertise, ease and with flair.

Strong winds, dry grass, high temperatures and more,

are fuel to the fires and make them roar.

Homes for people and wild animals too, are destroyed in the terrible madness.

Now they are homeless….it's true.

Firefighters do their best to keep people and animals out of harm's way.

They always come to the rescue and they truly do "save the day"!

So the next time you see the firefighters, tell them "thank you"……..for the job of

stopping fires is difficult, but that is what they do!

Firefighters risk their lives each time they go to a fire. They run the risk of getting burned, debris falling on them, or smoke inhalation. They must fight fires in the rain, sleet, snow, and even in windy conditions. They fight fires from the inside and outside of buildings, in the woods, and forests as well.

Although firemen wear protective clothing, there are still risks. Deciding which strategy to use to best fight a fire often requires quick thinking and prior knowledge. Firefighters spend weeks away from their families because they are required to live at the station when they are on duty assignment.

Waiting for the fire alarm to sound is always in the back of a firefighter's mind. Once that call comes in, the adrenaline begins flowing, and the mental process of firefighting begins. Quickly suiting up for the mission and actually departing for the fire is when the stress heightens. Finally, seeing the fire and the magnitude of it brings about even more stress!

Wow, what a dangerous and stressful job!

"So the next time you see firefighters, tell them Thank you! …. for the job of stopping fires is difficult, but that is what they do!"

Firefighters

Fires can be fierce, and they have such a treacherous,
yet colorful glow...
which makes the job of a firefighter very challenging
you know.
Firefighters battle fires on land and in the air,
for flying high would give me such a horrible scare.
They seem to fight fires with such expertise,
ease, and with flair.
Strong winds, dry grass, high temperatures, and more,
are fuel to the fires and make them roar.
Homes for people and wild animals too,
are destroyed in the terrible madness.
Now they are homeless…. it's true.
Firefighters do their best to keep people and animals
out of harm's way.
They always come to the rescue,
and they truly do "save the day"!

The next time you see the firefighters,
tell them "Thank you."
For the job of stopping fires is difficult,
but that is what they do!

Words cannot express my gratitude for our military forces, and the sacrifices they and their families make. As the wife of a retired military service member, I am grateful for the many opportunities that my family has had visiting countries that we read about in history books and travel magazines. It was amazing.

Experiencing life in other countries and immersing ourselves in other cultural experiences has refined us and broadened our awareness beyond the borders of the United States. I will always cherish those memories.

When there were temporary duty missions or field problems that took my husband away from the family for a while, we missed him, but we always found something to do to keep us occupied. Never did a day go by that we did not pray. This is what kept our family together, and prayer kept us safe.

During war times, our military families, personal families, and friends grew closer together. Support was what kept us positive about our loved one's return. Through it all, God brought us together again!

"Thank you, military forces, for all you do!"

Military Tribute

Whether you are in the Army, Air Force, Navy,
Coast Guard, or Marines,
we know you mean business
when you show up on the scene.

Risking your lives, when you answer the call.
For this reason, I want to thank you all!

Whether on active duty or retired,
you were the best qualified for your job,
so you were hired.

Leaving your families at home to wait for your return,
and for that, my admiration and respect, you have earned.

When wars break out and loved ones must go,
let's remind them in a special way that we love them so.

Knowing that their lives are so precious to us...
still they go off to fight the war with little or no fuss.

We pray for safe travels and for a safe return...
and while you are away,
a candle in our windows we will burn.

"Why burn a candle," you might ask?
Because fighting a war is dangerous
and it's a very difficult task!

This is a way to show our love and support,
for a war that we pray our service members
will be able to abort.

Many thanks to all of You, for all that you do.
I know your loyalty to our country is tried and true.
Without a doubt, you proudly represent
the red, white, and blue!

Me, The Poet

I am a self-proclaimed poet…

And I am announcing it so that you too will know it!

As I try to think of things to say,

with no hesitation, the words seem to come into my mind right away.

Writing poetry for most is not very easy at all,

But for me, in this area, I have received God's call.

What will I write about today?

First, I must listen to God and allow Him to give me the words to say.

Most importantly, I cannot forget to pray for God's guidance each and every day.

Oh yes, I must faithfully do my part, because writing poetry is truly a work of art.

What else can I say? My poetry speaks for itself.

I am a poet….

Me the poet!

Me, The Poet

I am a self-proclaimed poet...
And I am announcing it so that you too will know it!
As I try to think of things to say,
with no hesitation, the words seem to come into my mind right away.
Writing poetry for most is not very easy at all,
but for me, in this area, I have received God's call.
What will I write about today?
First, I must listen to God
and allow Him to give me the words to say.
Most importantly, I cannot forget to pray for God's guidance each and every day.
Oh yes, I must faithfully do my part, because writing poetry is truly a work of art.
What else can I say?
My poetry speaks for itself.
I am a poet....
Me, the poet!

My Custom Symbol

The Greek symbol for the number 4 is δ.

The number 4 is the symbol of totality, and it is considered the root of all things. It represents the union of the three persons of the Holy Trinity into only One Being. The number 4 symbolizes the family and is considered as another image of the number 1. The triangle represents symbolically the square of the cross, and it is the number of balance. The number 4 is used 279 times in the Bible and symbolizes building a strong foundation. Number 4 is the number of stability, order, and completion of justice.

The Triangles mean: The three distinct angles combine to make one complete figure, symbolizing the Holy Trinity. Triangles also represent: gender, creativity, harmony, proportion, ascension, manifestation, illumination, integration, and culmination. If the triangle is point-up this often represents a strong foundation or stability. Therefore, this means that the triangle is firmly placed on a solid base. The triangle represents the Trinity: The Father, Son, and Holy Ghost.

* **The Symbol:** The four triangles symbolize my husband, daughter, son, and myself. It represents our belief in the Holy Trinity and our strength because of the firm foundation on which we stand...The Father, The Son, and The Holy Spirit.

The colors of the symbol represent:

~The color **Amber** is only found in the KJV Book of Ezekiel and is used to demonstrate God's illuminous and immediate presence.

~The color **Blue** is used very often in the Old Testament as a symbol of wealth.

~The color **Grey** is used to denote old age and a long life.

~The color **Green** primarily depicts plant life as a symbol of natural growth and life.

~The color **White** is a color of purity and righteousness.

~The color **Red** is used throughout the Scriptures. Its primary association in this symbol represents the blood that Jesus shed for us on Calvary.

About the Author

Dr. Jan D. Johnson is a native of North Carolina, born to Mr. and Mrs. Darius Johnson, now deceased.

Jan also has one biological sister, Berta, and many sisters and brothers in Christ. Jan loves God and shares her love for Him eagerly with others. She has traveled extensively throughout the United States and abroad with her family because her husband, Robert Johnson, of 34 years is a retired military veteran. She has two very blessed and amazing adult children, a son, Robert II and a daughter, Robyn, with divinely inspired visions and purposes for their lives.

Jan is a graduate of Liberty University, Lynchburg, Virginia (Doctorate), Fayetteville State University, Fayetteville, North Carolina (Masters), Hampton University, Hampton, Virginia (Bachelors) and E.E. Smith High School, Fayetteville, North Carolina. She holds many certifications and enjoys her current employment opportunity as Math Instructional Support Specialist at her school on Ft. Bragg, North Carolina.

Divinely inspired through "Cultural Arts", Jan initiated this ministry in her church, Second Baptist Church in North Carolina, where her pastor is Rev. Dr. Ivory Swann. Jan, along with her daughter, Robyn, started the first "Praise

Dance Team" ministry in her church as well. It is Jan's belief that giving praise, glory, and honor to God is significant when one can witness God's awesomeness through the "gifts" and "talents" in which He has blessed us.

Jan's vision is that through her writing others will be inspired, uplifted, and renewed as they come to experience the awesomeness of God. Jan's desire is that others will see the impact that God has made in her life and be so inclined as to follow Him as well.

Scripture Reference

John 13:34 (KVJ)
A new commandment I give unto you, That ye love one another; as I have loved you, that ye also love one another.

Proverbs 3:17 (KJV)
Her ways are ways of pleasantness, and all her paths are peace.

Matthew 12:50 (KJV)
For whosoever shall do the will of my Father which is in heaven, the same is my brother, and sister, and mother.

Galatians 3:26 (KJV)
"For ye are all the children of God by faith in Christ Jesus."

Revelation 19:6-7(KJV)
6. And I heard as it were the voice of a great multitude, and as the voice of many waters, and as the voice of mighty thunderings, saying, Hallelujah! For the Lord God Almighty reigns.
7. Let us rejoice and be glad and give him glory! For the wedding of the Lamb has come, and his bride has made herself ready.

Proverbs 3:5-6 (KJV)
5 Trust in the LORD with all thine heart; and lean not unto thine own understanding.
6 In all thy ways acknowledge him, and he shall direct thy paths.

Isaiah 43:2 King James Version (KJV)
When thou passest through the waters, I will be with thee; and through the rivers, they shall not overflow thee: when thou walkest through the fire, thou shalt not be burned; neither shall the flame kindle upon thee.

Isaiah 14:24 (KJV)
The LORD of hosts hath sworn, saying, Surely as I have thought, so shall it come to pass; and as I have purposed, so shall it stand

Romans 8:11-12 (KJV)
11 But if the Spirit of him that raised up Jesus from the dead dwell in you, he that raised up Christ from the dead shall also quicken your mortal bodies by his Spirit that dwelleth in you.
12 Therefore, brethren, we are debtors, not to the flesh, to live after the flesh.

Joshua 1:9 (KJV)
Have not I commanded thee? Be strong and of a good courage; be not afraid, neither be thou dismayed: for the LORD thy God is with thee whithersoever thou goest.

John 10:9-11 (KJV)
9 I am the door: by me if any man enter in, he shall be saved, and shall go in and out, and find pasture.
10 The thief cometh not, but for to steal, and to kill, and to destroy: I am come that they might have life, and that they might have it more abundantly.
11 I am the good shepherd: the good shepherd giveth his life for the sheep.

The Butterfly Typeface Publishing House Co.

The Butterfly Typeface Publishing House Company is a full service professional publishing company. Our goal is to 'spread a message' of inspiration, imagination and intrigue in all that we do.

Whether you hire us to edit, ghostwrite, publish (books & magazines) or web design, you can be guaranteed exemplary customer service, fairness and quality.

Our vision, under God's leadership, is to serve and assist in the healing of the heart, mind and soul of *all* people we encounter with integrity, intentional influence and positive purpose.

"We make good GREAT!"

Iris M. Williams – Owner
The Butterfly Typeface Publishing House Co
Little Rock Arkansas

www.butterflytypeface.com

www.ingramcontent.com/pod-product-compliance
Lightning Source LLC
Chambersburg PA
CBHW042340150426
43196CB00001B/2